Published in the UK by
POWERFRESH Limited
3 Gray Street
Northampton
NN1 3QQ

Telephone 44 01604 30996
Facsimile 44 01604 21013

Cover and interior illustration Anthony Hutchings

Cover and interior layout Powerfresh

IT'S NO FUN BEING A MOTHER
ISBN 1 874125 37 6

Printed in the UK by Avalon Print Northampton
        Powerfresh October 1994

TITLES BY POWERFRESH

CRINKLED 'N' WRINKLED
DRIVEN CRAZY
OH NO ITS XMAS AGAIN
TRUE LOVE
IT'S A BOY
IT'S A GIRL
NOW WE ARE 40
FUNNY SIDE OF 40 HIM
FUNNY SIDE OF 40 HER
FUNNY SIDE OF 50 HIM
FUNNY SIDE OF 50 HER
FUNNY SIDE OF GOLF
FUNNY SIDE OF 60'S
FUNNY SIDE OF SEX
GERRY ATRIC'S GAG BOOK
THE COMPLETE WIMPS GUIDE TO SEX
THE COMPLETE BASTARDS GUIDE TO BUSINESS SURVIVAL
THE COMPLETE BASTARDS GUIDE TO SPORT
THE COMPLETE BASTARDS GUIDE TO GOLF
THE COMPLETE BASTARDS GUIDE TO LIFE
THE COMPLETE BASTARDS GUIDE TO SEX
MALCOM
KEEP FIT WITH YOUR CAT
THE OFFICE FROM HELL
MONSTERS
MARITAL BLISS AND OTHER OXYMORONS
THE ART OF SLOBOLOGY
IT'S NO FUN BEING A MOTHER
THE DEFINITIVE GUIDE TO VASECTOMY
PMT CRAZED

ALL TITLES RETAIL AT   £2.99